I SPOT OVALS

first concepts

BY NATALIE HUMPHREY

Gareth Stevens
PUBLISHING

Ovals are everywhere! The egg is an oval.

The mirror is an oval.

The plate is an oval.

The watermelon is an oval.

The rug is an oval.

11

The lemon is an oval.

13

The balloon is an oval.

15

The kiwi is an oval.

The soap is an oval.

19

The grape is an oval.

21

Can you spot the oval?

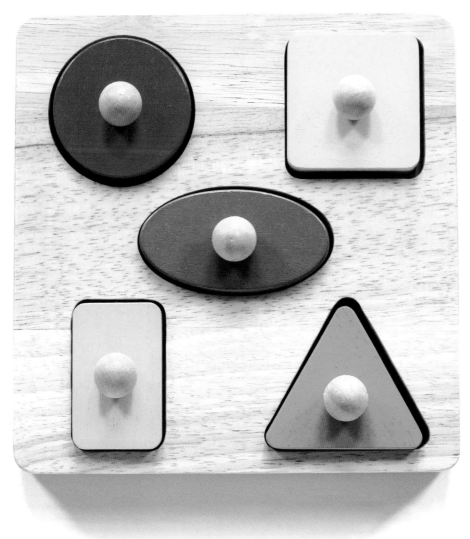

23

Please visit our website, www.garethstevens.com. For a free color catalog of all our high-quality books, call toll free 1-800-542-2595 or fax 1-877-542-2596.

Library of Congress Cataloging-in-Publication Data
Names: Humphrey, Natalie, author.
Title: I spot ovals / Natalie Humphrey.
Description: Buffalo, New York : Gareth Stevens Publishing, [2025] |
Series: I spot shapes | Includes index.
Identifiers: LCCN 2023044266 (print) | LCCN 2023044267 (ebook) | ISBN 9781538291740 (library binding) | ISBN 9781538291733 (paperback) | ISBN 9781538291757 (ebook)
Subjects: LCSH: Ovals–Juvenile literature. | Shapes–Juvenile literature. | Form perception–Juvenile literature.
Classification: LCC QA483 .H86 2025 (print) | LCC QA483 (ebook) | DDC 516/.154–dc23/eng/20231031
LC record available at https://lccn.loc.gov/2023044266 LC ebook record available at https://lccn.loc.gov/2023044267

Published in 2025 by
Gareth Stevens Publishing
2544 Clinton Street
West Seneca, NY 14224

Designer: Leslie Taylor
Editor: Natalie Humphrey

Photo credits: Cover daseaford/Shutterstock.com; p. 3 1exey/Shutterstock.com; p. 5 cheezzii/Shutterstock.com; p. 7 (plate) Theeradech Sanin/Shutterstock.com, (table) Seregam/Shutterstock.com; p. 9 Africa Studio/Shutterstock.com; p. 11 Ayman alakhras/Shutterstock.com; p. 13 Maks Narodenko/Shutterstock.com; p. 15 Lens7/Shutterstock.com; p. 17 Spayder pauk_79/Shutterstock.com; p. 19 Mitrofanova/Shutterstock.com; p. 21 Tim UR/Shutterstock.com; p. 23 Heidi Becker/Shutterstock.com.

Printed in the United States of America

CPSIA compliance information: Batch #CSGS25: For further information contact Gareth Stevens, New York, New York at 1-800-542-2595.

Find us on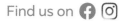